Published by MTNWalker Media, L.L.C.
6080 South Hulen, Suite 360, PMB 101
Fort Worth, Texas 76132

AlexisFaere.com

ISBN 978-1-958786-04-8

Stayin' In Touch Series

Stayin' In Touch
Volume 2 - Positive
Volume 3 - Negative
Volume 4 - Peaceful
Volume 5 - Corporate
Volume 6 - Elder
Volume 7 - Parental
Volume 8 - Friend
Volume 9 - Gratitude
Volume 10 - Grief

Enjoy the entire series…

Here's a little secret! If you want some examples of how to write about emotions, find my personalized expressions on:

AlexisFaere.com

We all feel a variety of emotions in the moments of each day. This journal is intended to provide a safe place for you to acknowledge different corporate emotions, where they come from, what they feel like, and what you can learn about them. Sometimes it is simply helpful to put a name to any given feeling.

Emotions are a part of our whole self - whether it feels good or not. Recognizing your feelings is part of accepting who you are as a person in this world.

Perhaps you can find a way for any given feeling to function on your behalf, thus allowing it to be present, or less present in your life. I invite you to play with each emotion in a way that helps to grow you into the person you want to be.

Feel free to skip around, there is no need to follow this journal from front to back. Pick a represented feeling that speaks to you on any given day and explore it, draw it, find pictures that express it, or write about it. Allow your emotions to be felt, heard, acknowledged, and understood.

Today is all about *appreciated*...

Date: _____

Location: _____

Explain your *appreciated* feeling: _____

_____

_____

_____

Where I feel it in my body: _____

_____

What I've learned today about feeling *appreciated*:

_____

_____

_____

What does your *appreciated* feeling look like?

A story about *appreciated* you'd like to remember:
(Draw, write, paste a picture, or whatever you'd like to add.)

Today is all about *bored...*

Date: _____

Location: _____

Explain your *bored* feeling: _____

_____

_____

_____

Where I feel it in my body: _____

_____

What I've learned today about feeling *bored*:

_____

_____

_____

What does your *bored* feeling look like?

A story about *bored* you'd like to remember:

(Draw, write, paste a picture, or whatever you'd like to add.)

Today is all about *confident…*

Date: _____

Location: _____

Explain your *confident* feeling: _____

_____

_____

_____

Where I feel it in my body: _____

_____

What I've learned today about feeling *confident*:

_____

_____

_____

What does your *confident* feeling look like?

A story about *confident* you'd like to remember:
(Draw, write, paste a picture, or whatever you'd like to add.)

Today is all about *dread*...

Date: _____

Location: _____

Explain your *dread* feeling: _____

_____

_____

_____

Where I feel it in my body: _____

_____

What I've learned today about feeling *dread*:

_____

_____

_____

What does your *dread* feeling look like?

A story about *dread* you'd like to remember:
(Draw, write, paste a picture, or whatever you'd like to add.)

Today is all about *eager*...

Date: _____

Location: _____

Explain your *eager* feeling: _____

_____

_____

_____

Where I feel it in my body: _____

_____

What I've learned today about feeling *eager*:

_____

_____

_____

What does your *eager* feeling look like?

A story about *eager* you'd like to remember:
(*Draw, write, paste a picture, or whatever you'd like to add.*)

Today is all about *fraud...*

Date: _____

Location: _____

Explain your *fraud* feeling: _____

_____

_____

_____

Where I feel it in my body: _____

_____

What I've learned today about feeling *fraud*:

_____

_____

_____

What does your *fraud* feeling look like?

A story about *fraud* you'd like to remember:
(*Draw, write, paste a picture, or whatever you'd like to add.*)

Today is all about *greedy*…

Date: _____

Location: _____

Explain your *greedy* feeling: _____

_____

_____

_____

Where I feel it in my body: _____

_____

What I've learned today about feeling *greedy*:

_____

_____

_____

What does your *greedy* feeling look like?

A story about greedy you'd like to remember:

(Draw, write, paste a picture, or whatever you'd like to add.)

Today is all about *honored…*

Date: _____

Location: _____

Explain your *honored* feeling: _____

_____

_____

_____

Where I feel it in my body: _____

_____

What I've learned today about feeling *honored*: _____

_____

_____

What does your *honored* feeling look like?

A story about *honored* you'd like to remember:
(*Draw, write, paste a picture, or whatever you'd like to add.*)

Today is all about *insecure*...

Date: _____

Location: _____

Explain your *insecure* feeling: _____

_____

_____

_____

Where I feel it in my body: _____

_____

What I've learned today about feeling *insecure*:

_____

_____

_____

What does your *insecure* feeling look like?

A story about *insecure* you'd like to remember:

(Draw, write, paste a picture, or whatever you'd like to add.)

Today is all about *judgmental...*

Date: _____

Location: _____

Explain your *judgmental* feeling: _____

_____

_____

_____

Where I feel it in my body: _____

_____

What I've learned today about feeling *judgmental*:

_____

_____

_____

What does your *judgmental* feeling look like?

A story about *judgmental* you'd like to remember:

(Draw, write, paste a picture, or whatever you'd like to add.)

Today is all about *kind...*

Date: _____

Location: _____

Explain your *kind* feeling: _____

_____

_____

_____

Where I feel it in my body: _____

_____

What I've learned today about feeling *kind*:

_____

_____

_____

What does your *kind* feeling look like?

A story about *kind* you'd like to remember:
(Draw, write, paste a picture, or whatever you'd like to add.)

Today is all about *loyal*...

Date: _____

Location: _____

Explain your *loyal* feeling: _____

_____

_____

_____

Where I feel it in my body: _____

_____

What I've learned today about feeling *loyal*:

_____

_____

_____

What does your *loyal* feeling look like?

A story about *loyal* you'd like to remember:

(Draw, write, paste a picture, or whatever you'd like to add.)

Today is all about *miffed*...

Date: _____

Location: _____

Explain your *miffed* feeling: _____

_____

_____

_____

Where I feel it in my body: _____

_____

What I've learned today about feeling *miffed*:

_____

_____

_____

What does your *miffed* feeling look like?

A story about *miffed* you'd like to remember:
(Draw, write, paste a picture, or whatever you'd like to add.)

Today is all about *negative...*

Date: _____

Location: _____

Explain your *negative* feeling: _____

_____

_____

_____

Where I feel it in my body: _____

_____

What I've learned today about feeling *negative*:

_____

_____

_____

What does your *negative* feeling look like?

A story about *negative* you'd like to remember:
(Draw, write, paste a picture, or whatever you'd like to add.)

Today is all about *overloaded...*

Date: _____

Location: _____

Explain your *overloaded* feeling: _____

_____

_____

_____

Where I feel it in my body: _____

_____

What I've learned today about feeling *overloaded*:

_____

_____

_____

What does your *overloaded* feeling look like?

A story about *overloaded* you'd like to remember:
(Draw, write, paste a picture, or whatever you'd like to add.)

Today is all about *possessive...*

Date: _____

Location: _____

Explain your *possessive* feeling: _____

_____

_____

_____

Where I feel it in my body: _____

_____

What I've learned today about feeling *possessive:*

_____

_____

_____

What does your *possessive* feeling look like?

A story about *possessive* you'd like to remember:
(Draw, write, paste a picture, or whatever you'd like to add.)

Today is all about *queasy*...

Date: _____

Location: _____

Explain your *queasy* feeling: _____

_____

_____

_____

Where I feel it in my body: _____

_____

What I've learned today about feeling *queasy*:

_____

_____

_____

What does your *queasy* feeling look like?

A story about *queasy* you'd like to remember:
(*Draw, write, paste a picture, or whatever you'd like to add.*)

Today is all about *resigned*…

Date: _____

Location: _____

Explain your *resigned* feeling: _____

_____

_____

_____

Where I feel it in my body: _____

_____

What I've learned today about feeling *resigned*:

_____

_____

_____

What does your *resigned* feeling look like?

A story about *resigned* you'd like to remember:
(Draw, write, paste a picture, or whatever you'd like to add.)

Today is all about *stressed*…

Date: _____

Location: _____

Explain your *stressed* feeling: _____

_____

_____

_____

Where I feel it in my body: _____

_____

What I've learned today about feeling *stressed*:

_____

_____

_____

What does your *stressed* feeling look like?

A story about *stressed* you'd like to remember:
(Draw, write, paste a picture, or whatever you'd like to add.)

Today is all about *threatened*...

Date: _____

Location: _____

Explain your *threatened* feeling: _____

_____

_____

_____

Where I feel it in my body: _____

_____

What I've learned today about feeling *threatened*:

_____

_____

_____

What does your *threatened* feeling look like?

A story about *threatened* you'd like to remember:
(Draw, write, paste a picture, or whatever you'd like to add.)

Today is all about *useful*...

Date: _____

Location: _____

Explain your *useful* feeling: _____

_____

_____

_____

Where I feel it in my body: _____

_____

What I've learned today about feeling *useful*:

_____

_____

_____

What does your *useful* feeling look like?

A story about *useful* you'd like to remember:

(Draw, write, paste a picture, or whatever you'd like to add.)

Today is all about *venal*…

Date: _____

Location: _____

Explain your *venal* feeling: _____

_____

_____

_____

Where I feel it in my body: _____

_____

What I've learned today about feeling *venal*:

_____

_____

_____

What does your *venal* feeling look like?

A story about *venal* you'd like to remember:
(Draw, write, paste a picture, or whatever you'd like to add.)

Today is all about *worried*...

Date: _____

Location: _____

Explain your *worried* feeling: _____

_____

_____

_____

Where I feel it in my body: _____

_____

What I've learned today about feeling *worried*:

_____

_____

_____

What does your *worried* feeling look like?

A story about *worried* you'd like to remember:
(Draw, write, paste a picture, or whatever you'd like to add.)

Today is all about *xenial...*

Date: _____

Location: _____

Explain your *xenial* feeling: _____

_____

_____

_____

Where I feel it in my body: _____

_____

What I've learned today about feeling *xenial*:

_____

_____

_____

What does your *xenial* feeling look like?

A story about *xenial* you'd like to remember:
(Draw, write, paste a picture, or whatever you'd like to add.)

Today is all about *yielding*...

Date: _____

Location: _____

Explain your *yielding*: _____

_____

_____

_____

Where I feel it in my body: _____

_____

What I've learned today about *yielding*:

_____

_____

_____

What does your *yielding* look like?

A story about *yielding* you'd like to remember:
(Draw, write, paste a picture, or whatever you'd like to add.)

Today is all about *zany*...

Date: _____

Location: _____

Explain your *zany* feeling: _____

_____

_____

_____

Where I feel it in my body: _____

_____

What I've learned today about feeling *zany*:

_____

_____

_____

What does your *zany* feeling look like?

A story about *zany* you'd like to remember:
(Draw, write, paste a picture, or whatever you'd like to add.)

CPSIA information can be obtained
at www.ICGtesting.com
Printed in the USA
LVHW080448021022
729737LV00001B/4